The Rattlesnake Looks for Food

Written by
Tom Pipher

Illustrated by
Clive Taylor

The rattlesnake
looks for food.
The little mouse
looks for food, too.

The rattlesnake
can eat the little mouse.
The little mouse
cannot eat the rattlesnake.

The rattlesnake
hears the little mouse.
The rattlesnake
smells the little mouse.
The rattlesnake
sees the little mouse.

Can the little mouse
hear the rattlesnake?
No! The little mouse
cannot hear the rattlesnake.

Can the little mouse
smell the rattlesnake?
No! The little mouse
cannot smell the rattlesnake.

Can the little mouse
see the rattlesnake?
Yes! The little mouse
can see the rattlesnake.

Can the rattlesnake get the little mouse? No! The little mouse jumps up and runs away.

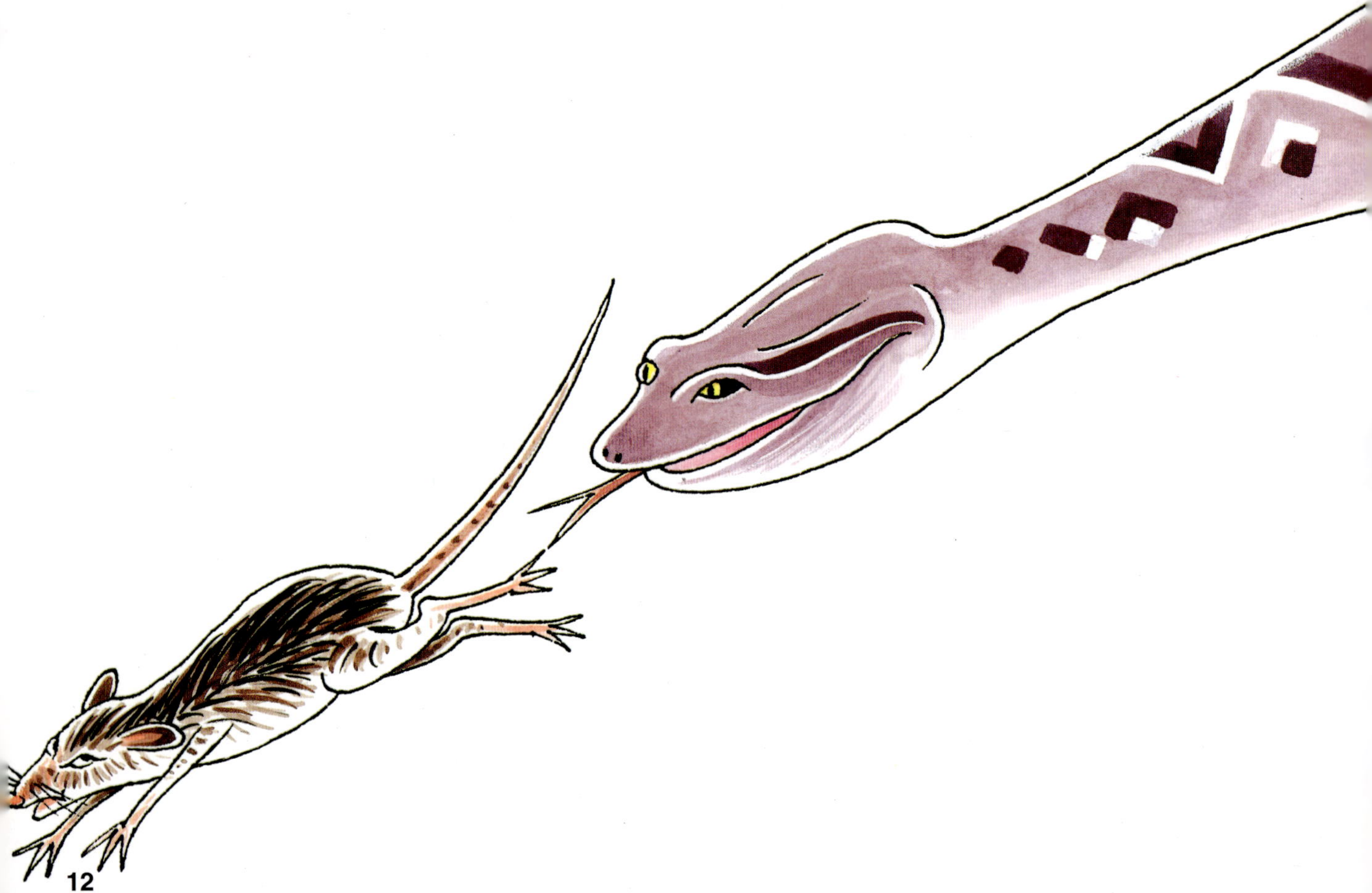